THE PROJECT

by Ian Buckley

Published by Playdead Press 2019

© Ian Buckley 2019

Ian Buckley has asserted his rights under the Copyright, Design and Patents Act, 1988, to be identified as the author of this work.

A CIP catalogue record for this book is available from the British Library.

ISBN 978-1-910067-75-8

Caution
All rights whatsoever in this play are strictly reserved and application for performance should be sought through the author before rehearsals begin. No performance may be given unless a license has been obtained.

This book is sold subject to the condition that it shall not by way of trade or otherwise, be lent, resold, hired out, or otherwise circulated without the publisher's prior consent in any form of binding or cover other than that in which it is published and without a similar condition including this condition being imposed on the subsequent purchaser.

Playdead Press
www.playdeadpress.com

The Project was first produced at The White Bear Theatre, London, March 5th – 23rd 2019, with the following cast:

CONRAD SCHAFFER	**Mike Duran**
ANNA HILMANN	**Faye Maughan**
MILLIE HILMANN	**Eloise Jones**
PETER WEISS	**Nick Delvalle**
VICTOR GERRIN	**Lloyd Morris**
ETTE HILMANN	**Cate Morris**

Director	**Anthony Shrubsall**
Writer	**Ian Buckley**
Designer	**Sarah Baker**
Stage & Technical Management	**Alistair Warr**
Lighting Desiger	**Chuma**
Producer	**Ian Buckley for RedNeedle**
Casting	**Sarah Lawrie**
Publicity	**Kevin Wilson PR**
Social Media	**MyTheatreMates**

Ian Buckley | Writer

Ian went to Christ's College Cambridge from the Elliott Comprehensive in Putney. He gained an Honours degree in English Literature plus a soccer blue for good measure. He continued his studies at the University of Kent where he gained an MA researching the works of Sean O'Casey.

Having spent most of his school/university years analysing and assessing the works of other playwrights, Ian decided it was time to become a playwright himself. It's what he's been doing ever since.

Ian has had a number of plays performed on the London fringe: *Realife TV* (2016), *The Moment We Met* (2015), *Picasso's Artful Occupation* (2014) and *The Tailors' Last Stand* (2013) (all RedNeedle Productions at Barons Court Theatre, London); *Keeping Faith* (The Kings Head); *First Timers* (The Dukes Head); *Suits & Blouses* (The Room at The Orange Tree); *Down The River* (Theatre Royal Stratford East, touring show); *Tainted Love* (The Young Actors Theatre). His last play, *James Bonney MP* was staged at The White Bear Theatre, Kennington in 2017.

He's been shortlisted for the following playwriting competitions: the Verity Bargate Award; the Maddermarket Award; The Bruntwood Prize (long-shortlisted with *The Return*) and the Brockley Jack 'Write Now Three' competition.

He's had a play on BBC Radio Four: *Changing Gear*, re-broadcast in translation on Hessische Rundfunk in Germany, who also broadcast *The Revolutionary*.

He was granted an Arts Council Writer's Bursary to complete his play *Dr Richter & Pero* – about the first ever meeting of Lenin and Trotsky in London in 1902

The Project is Ian's second play to be staged at The White Bear Theatre.

Writer's Notes | How The Play Came About

What kick started me into writing *The Project* was a previous play of mine – *Picasso's Artful Occupation*. As I focused on this great artist's life in Paris under Nazi occupation, it led me into a wider reading of how the Nazi killing machine operated Europe-wide.

I came across Westerbork quite by chance. I knew names like Auschwitz, Belsen, Sobibor, but I'd never heard of Westerbork. I'd also never made the distinction between a concentration camp (for killing or working to death) and a holding camp like Westerbork (for registering, filing, sorting). The latter were rightfully labelled *'the ante-rooms to the gates of hell'*

I didn't know that life in these holding camps was tough and unpleasant, but infinitely better than the onwards destination waiting for their inmates. In Westerbork they were 'allowed' to play sports, attend keep-fit classes, rehearse and present cabaret and engage in other cultural pursuits. They had a huge well-staffed hospital-wing. However the 'they' who could enjoy these things (if enjoy is the right word) were normally the minority of longer-stay inmates who helped – under severe duress – to run the camp. The vast majority of Dutch Jews came into the camp, were registered and left soon after on the weekly transport to the frightening East.

Part of the reason I felt so impelled to write *The Project* was because of its relevance for our times, especially in the light of the re-growth of fascism in Europe today. It's important to know where fascism/nazism always ends up – in huge societal destruction and the victimisation and destruction of minority groups. 1940's Nazi Germany is a paradigm for this process and Westerbork Camp one example (and not the worst) of the killing machine cranking up to do its deadly duty.

When we see Anna and Millie and Peter and Ette and Victor and we understand where they ended up, we need to learn lessons and ensure it never ever happens again.

THE PROJECT
by Ian Buckley

CAST:

Conrad Schaffer: 38, uniformed, smart, director of Camp, wears belt with gun, German SS

Victor Gerrin: 43, master of ceremonies, star of cabaret, theatre producer, Jewish

Anna Hilmann: 29, entertainer, cabaret artiste, shapely figure, muscular & elegant, Jewish - elder sister of Millie.

Millie Hilmann: 27, entertainer, singer of popular songs, spiritualist & healer - Jewish - younger sister of Anna.

Peter Weiss: 34, comic, poet, Jewish,

Ette Hilmann: 63, mother of Anna and Millie, housewife and mother in a million, Jewish.

The action takes place in Westerbork. A drab, enclosed transit camp in north eastern Holland in 1943.

SCENE ONE

A large wood-built hall

Early evening

Victor is miming a comedy routine. He acts two parts, switching characters by stepping from left to right. He speaks lines to himself. Comic effect.

Enter Anna

VICTOR: Anna at last. Put me out of my misery. How did it go? What did he say, what did you say back?

ANNA: Chit chat...that's all.

VICTOR: Anna I asked *how* it went.

ANNA: And I told you...

VICTOR: Chit chat's not enough.

ANNA: I can't say.

VICTOR: Why not?

ANNA: Because I promised I wouldn't.

VICTOR: A Jew is not obliged to keep a promise to their jailor.

ANNA: Isn't a promise a promise?

VICTOR: ...They lie to us all the time.

ANNA: I don't know that many jailors.

VICTOR: ...Believe me they do. All the time. So why should we keep our word to them? Anna I need to know.

ANNA: If I tell you and it gets out...

VICTOR: It won't get out.

Victor grips Anna's left hand in his right hand

ANNA: He wants to meet me.

VICTOR: Alone?

ANNA: ...Yes.

VICTOR: He's hooked, he's hooked!

ANNA: ...To dance for him.

VICTOR: Of course you said yes?

ANNA: No...

VICTOR: You didn't? My god, my christ why not you must.

ANNA: ...I don't know if I want to Victor.

VICTOR: You need to find the right dance.

ANNA: You're not listening.

VICTOR: ...One that will lead him on so far but no further...

ANNA: *If* I accept.

VICTOR: The erotic to stir his loins, the comic to cool them off.

ANNA: ...I'm not a femme fatale. I'm not sure I know how to carry this off.

VICTOR: Anna, I hope you don't think I'm taking you for granted.

ANNA:	Who knows what you're taking me for Victor?
VICTOR:	Did he say where you can meet? Does he want me to help set it up?
ANNA:	I'm to give him a sign... *if* I agree. Don't ask – I'm not telling you what it is.
VICTOR:	Cunning. Him I mean.
	If he can't do it in total secrecy he won't.
	Typical Nazi - wants to mix with Jews but doesn't want to be seen to.
ANNA:	I can't see where it's going to lead...
VICTOR:	I'll tell you. Some fun, some innocent pleasure and a growing influence over CS.

Enter Peter

He sinks to the floor, dirty & exhausted

ANNA:	Peter? Where were you today?
PETER:	Digging ditches.
VICTOR:	Why on earth were you doing that?
PETER:	They need them dug?
ANNA:	What happened to foil-stripping?
PETER:	I can wield a pick and shovel and all-heart Brooks thought I needed a change.
ANNA:	What's it got to do with Brooks?
PETER:	I was setting a bad example to the foil-strippers he said. He reported me.

VICTOR: Hut-leaders – always bastards when they've just been promoted.

PETER: And you Anna? How did you get on?

ANNA: ...Okay.

PETER: Only okay?

ANNA: ...He was pleasant...

PETER: Beware him when he's pleasant. He's weaving his web.

VICTOR: No we're weaving our web, let him beware.

Enter Millie. Hallos exchanged

ANNA: Millie? You've not been digging ditches as well?

MILLIE: Ditches?

ANNA: ...Like Peter. They've promoted him to ditch-digger first-class.

MILLIE: No I... I...

ANNA: Millie love? What's wrong?

Millie throws her arms around Anna

MILLIE: Her name... it's on the list.

ANNA: Whose name?

MILLIE: Mum's...

ANNA: Which list?

MILLIE: The Tuesday one. Someone whispered at work... a friend of Pearl's lady-friend. She'd heard a rumour... I ran to Pearl, to check. At first he wouldn't say. How dare someone pass on private information, this was against normal planning... no one should know before... blah blah. I begged him, I pleaded with him. I said I wouldn't leave his office till he told me. So he did. He even showed me the name.

ANNA: ...I don't understand? Mum's ill. She's in a hospital ward.

MILLIE: I went back to the hut. I touched every one of my crystals. Put them at every angle. I felt nothing. Not the faintest good force.

VICTOR: You need to talk to people...maybe especially CS.

ANNA: Can you speak to him Victor? For us?

MILLIE: If you do I'll love you for ever. I'll worship the ground you walk on.

VICTOR: We don't have a meeting planned till next week.

ANNA: That's too late. We have to speak to him now. The sooner the better.

VICTOR: What's a reason I can give for a meeting?

ANNA: (*Reflects*) ...We need more lights... ...or new costumes...?

VICTOR: That's it – the reason. A new costume for your new dance Anna.

PETER: What new dance?

Millie takes small polished crystal-stone from pocket, holds in hand

MILLIE: ...My stone feels warm. It likes this talk of a meeting with the Commandant. (*She holds polished pebble to her cheek, forehead, neck*)

PETER: I didn't know you had a new dance.

ANNA: Neither did I till Victor said I needed one five minutes ago. But needing one isn't having one.

VICTOR: CS wants Anna to dance for him...

PETER: (*To Anna*) ...Just you?

ANNA: There was no thought of hiding it from you Peter. We were going to tell you...

PETER: (*To Victor*) This is all your silly doing isn't it. Plotting and planning like this.

ANNA: I haven't said yes. (*To Victor*) Can't you talk to him about costumes in general and then ask if he'll help Mum?

VICTOR: Why miss the chance to boost an idea?

ANNA: When can you see him? There's so little time.

VICTOR: I can try now.

ANNA: Now. Yes. Let us know the minute you've got any news.

PETER: Boost what idea Victor?

VICTOR: (*To Anna*) Can I tell him you accept his invite?

ANNA: No you can't, you mustn't. I told you I promised him I wouldn't breathe a word.

VICTOR: (*Thinks*) I can say it so it looks like you haven't.

MILLIE: Tell us how, clever Victor.

VICTOR: ...I talk about costumes... move on to you, your mum, your distress... suggest if he could help her you'd be undyingly grateful. Then slip in like it's just hit me he could even ask you to dance and you couldn't say no.

ANNA: All I know is he mustn't think I've had anything to do with it.

VICTOR: He won't. I'll say it as if the idea's just dropped from the sky.

PETER: Like bird-shit?

VICTOR: Can I Anna?

ANNA: If you have to Victor. If you think it will help.

VICTOR: I'm sure it will.

PETER: Don't have anything to do with this Anna. It's risky and dangerous.

ANNA: What choice do I have Peter? I have to get Mother off the list. That's all I can think of. Nothing else counts.

END OF SCENE 1

SCENE TWO

The Hospital Wing – A Bed

Ette lies propped up on simple bed

Anna, Millie by bed

ETTE: Will you please not rush me. I'm breathless as it is. (*Breathes*) Pudding-face Pearl suddenly popped up - at four this morning. (*She points*) 'Wake up everybody! We're short this week. The following are therefore chosen...'

ANNA: But people in here aren't well.

ETTE: The numbers on the ward have to go down by half according to his lordship.

ANNA: What's he going to do? Wave a magic wand and cure them ready for travel?

MILLIE: Why do the numbers have to go down?

ETTE: Because our masters say too many of us here are missing their excursions which isn't fair on the others. Little do they know I've been praying for this for months.

ANNA: The months may be longer where they're sending you.

MILLIE: Anna's right Mum. Better to stay.

ETTE: My lovely daughters d'you think I love this place so much I can't bear to leave it?

MILLIE: No one loves this place but better the devil you know...

ANNA:	Some people think it'll be a lot worse when you leave.
ETTE:	I don't care if it is. No I do. For your father's sake.
ANNA:	We care too don't we Millie. For both your sakes... and that's why we want you to stay.
MILLIE:	We pray for Dad a hundred times a day. You mustn't think we've forgotten him.
ETTE:	Six months – one postcard... didn't even sound like him. If I go I can find him...
MILLIE:	You won't be much good to him if you're not fit,
ETTE:	...If there's a less practical man in the world I've not met him...
ANNA:	(*Joining in*) ...'You've not met him'... Yes we know we know. You've told us a thousand times.
ETTE:	...Always solving some problem in his beloved maths. He walks into doors his head's so full of formulae.
MILLIE:	You know what came to me today... like I knew it was the truth. Dad's found a friend where he is, who looks out for him.
ETTE:	He doesn't need a friend – he's got a wife.
ANNA:	...And you can go to him – when you're better. Patience and rest now. Here's the best place for it.
MILLIE:	Let me and Anna keep you here? Please?

ETTE: Don't tempt me. Think of your father. He's been through it, why shouldn't I?

ANNA: If Dad saw you now you know what he'd say? Stay. In that voice of his. Till you're well. He always thought of what was best for you.

ETTE: Why doesn't he write? He always did whenever he was away. I fall asleep wondering...

ANNA: Set yourself a goal. 'I'll go to Dad when I'm better'. You'll be no help to him weak.

ETTE: Sometimes I wonder... say he's...? And me not there to care for him?

ANNA: And no thinking morbid thoughts. They never lead to anything good.

MILLIE: Don't any of the prominents have news about Dad?

ETTE: Hah. We old ones aren't fools. We've got eyes. We work things out. Our bosses know no more than us about what happens to people who leave and if they did they wouldn't tell.

ANNA: Millie and I will work day and night to help you if you'll let us. (*Ette stays stubbornly silent*) Mother you know the choice. You come off the list or we go on. (*Ette nothing*)

MILLIE: Oh Mum please. Say yes. Please, please...

ANNA: It's one or the other.

ETTE: Don't threaten me Anna.

ANNA: I'm not threatening you. I'm telling you what Millie and I don't want to do but will have to do if you don't give us permission.

ETTE: Isn't she hard on me Millie?

MILLIE: She's thinking of you.

ETTE: Taking her side against me. Again.

MILLIE: A family's a circle Mum. Circles don't have sides.

ANNA: Can we then?

ETTE: Oh if you must. But if you don't manage it you're not to join me. You promise?

ANNA: We will manage it.

ETTE: If you don't promise I'll take back my yes.

ANNA: Okay yes.

ETTE: Promise?

ANNA: Promise.

ETTE: Millie?

MILLIE: I promise too.

ETTE: There. We've both made a compromise. And it was a lot harder for me than it was for you.

ANNA: Now that's settled I've brought a treat for you. (*Anna takes an orange from her pocket, peels it*) ...And I want you to eat it.

ETTE: You need it more...

ANNA: Vitamins Mum... build you up.

ETTE: ...To help you stay young.

ANNA: Open wide. (*Ready to pop segment in*)

ETTE: I will if we share. (*She shuts her mouth tight*)

ANNA: Each of us equal parts?

ETTE: Done.

Anna separates and hands out segments of orange. They share them three ways

MILLIE: And after we'll share my bread. (*Millie takes chunk of brown bread from pocket*) There's no mould.

ANNA: Here's to bread and orange fingers and then we must get working. Not a minute to lose.

END OF SCENE 2

SCENE THREE

A scruffy outside area within the perimeter fence

Shortly after previous scene

Schaffer comes to a halt, attention engrossed offstage. Victor tries to get his attention

VICTOR:	...She's not just anyone, she's the mother of a friend sir...
CS:	(*To a person off*) You there! Get back!
VICTOR:	An older lady...
CS:	Excuse me a moment.

CS takes revolver out of holster. Takes safety-catch off. Exits SR.

Crack of pistol. Short scream. Prolonged moaning

CS enters from SR, putting revolver in holster. He walks past victor, who tries not to look shocked, shouts offstage left

CS:	(*To someone off*) You there! Fetch a doctor. A doctor! Get a move on. It's urgent. (*Turns attention to Victor*) Now Gerrin...? You were saying...?
VICTOR:	This lovely old lady finds her name down for next Tuesday.
CS:	She's one of many then.
VICTOR:	The problem for her is that at present she's in the hospital wing.
CS:	Along with half the centre's residents you mean?

VICTOR:	(*Quiet voice*) Mrs Ette Hilmann. Anna's mother.
CS:	Ah. (*Thinks*) Did Anna ask you to come?
VICTOR:	Yes.
CS:	Why didn't she come herself?
VICTOR:	She's too embarrassed.
CS:	...Has she talked about me since you and I...?
VICTOR:	A lot.
CS:	(*Gratified*) Only to you I hope?
VICTOR:	Of course.
CS:	How d'you know?
VICTOR:	Know? Err... well... she said. 'I only talk about this to you Victor. I don't want the others to hear.'
CS:	Not her sister?
VICTOR:	Especially not her. Oh the green-eyed monster.
CS:	Not the comic?
VICTOR:	Peter? Not in a thousand years.
CS:	He likes Anna I've noticed. Does she like him?
VICTOR:	I've seen nothing to make me think that and I work closely with both.
CS:	So... what did she say about me?
VICTOR:	Her heart beats faster when she sees you.

CS:	That's good.
VICTOR:	She thinks you're handsome.
CS:	Better.
VICTOR:	She... admires your knowledge.
CS:	What knowledge is that?
VICTOR:	Of the cabaret world. She says you're an expert.
CS:	Um... anything else?
VICTOR:	If I was the man her heart beat faster for I'd be asking myself isn't that enough?
CS:	Nothing about dancing?
VICTOR:	Dancing...?
CS:	...For me?
VICTOR:	For you?
CS:	She's not referred to it in in any way?
VICTOR:	Why is it something you've...?
CS:	Just answer the question Gerrin.
VICTOR:	Not a word. But what a wonderful idea. Why didn't I think of it? Two young people, interests in common...
CS:	Yes, yes. Gerrin I'm busy.
VICTOR:	...About Anna's mother?
CS:	...Tilson?
VICTOR:	Hilmann. Ette.

CS: Anna can come and ask me in person.

VICTOR: Shall I tell her?

CS: Yes. (*Reflects*) Gerrin, I'm going to tell you something in confidence. You mustn't breathe a word.

VICTOR: I never betray a trust.

CS: (*Quiet*) ...I've suggested to Anna we meet. In private. I've given her time to think. If she says yes arrangements will need to be made. You can be our go-between.

VICTOR: I'm honoured.

CS: Not a word of this to Anna till I say.

VICTOR: Silence is the rule sir till you say.

CS: What you *can* do now is win her over to meeting me. Point out the advantages. Act as if it's coming from you, not me. You've got some influence with her haven't you?

VICTOR: She looks up to me personally. She depends on me professionally.

CS: ...How good it is to have powerful friends. What a stroke of luck to be noticed by them...

VICTOR: I'll start as soon as I get her on her own. I'll encourage her. I'll sing your praises.

CS: You can drop a hint – unofficial of course – that seeing me may help her mother...

VICTOR: I will. I'll drop that hint so subtly she'll hardly realise but the seed will be planted.

CS: I'll pop into rehearsal this evening. Please continue as if I'm not there. (*Seeing someone off*) That looks like the doctor. (*Shouts*) Doctor, that man there. (*CS points off*) Staunch the wound in his foot then get him to hospital. (*To Gerrin*) Ears tuned – I want to know what she says. And total secrecy. Absolute trust. Not a word to anyone or...

Lights down

END OF SCENE 3

SCENE FOUR

Well-furnished light, airy living-room in pleasant detached house outside the grounds of the centre

Two days later, a friday. 6.00 pm. Still just light

Armchairs, side-lamps – elegant with a hint of opulence

Outside a car draws up, car doors slam. Front-door open, footsteps

Enter CS followed by anna

CS goes to curtains, draws them shut, puts side lights on

CS: Sit down. Would you like a drink? I can offer whisky, martini, vodka...

ANNA: Thank you... after if I may.

CS goes to cabinet, pours himself a generous whisky, adds soda from syphon, sits

Anna stands, says nothing

CS: You'll be expected to sweep, dust surfaces, scrub pans...

ANNA: I'll do whatever's expected of me.

CS: If we meet in front of other residents, or other residents come to the house I'll treat you distantly. It won't mean anything.

ANNA: I understand.

CS: This evening won't be too long. The time it takes to set up the job. (*Walking to door USL and opening it*) You can change in here.

Anna stands. Exits into adjoining room

She leaves door very slightly ajar

CS stands. Sips drink

CS: Gerrin tells me your mother's down for next Tuesday's transport.

ANNA: (*Off*) Yes.

CS: And you're anxious?

ANNA: (*Off*) I'm hoping from the bottom of my heart some kind soul will see her removed.

CS: There are kind souls in the most unexpected places.

ANNA: (*Off*) Mother's so frail. A three-day journey's the last thing she needs.

CS: There are nurses and doctors with them.

ANNA: (*Off*) All the same we wish Mum could stay. She needs the care she gets here.

Anna re-enters room

She is dressed in flowing cotton dance dress, barefoot

CS: ...What a dress. You look amazing.

ANNA: I'm pleased if it pleases you.

CS: Will you dance then?

ANNA: Can I have music?

CS goes to turntable, puts vinyl on – popular dance tune

Anna dances – erotic and comic. Dance finishes

CS: (*Applauding*) Bravo. Superb.

ANNA: It had its faults. I've not had long to rehearse.

CS: I didn't notice. Sit down. Let me look at you.

Anna sits in armchair opposite CS. CS drinks her beauty in

Will you have a drink now?

ANNA: Water please.

CS: Just water?

ANNA: Alcohol stays on your breath. People wonder...

CS pours water into a glass for anna. Tops up his whisky

CS: To a dancer and a dance-lover.

ANNA: Long live the dance.

They drink

CS: I've seen you dance before. Six years ago to the month.

ANNA: I hope I didn't embarrass myself?

CS: The Black Swan Club in Central Street. I can even remember the dance. You were enticing a man into your arms but at the last moment he ran away.

ANNA: Sounds like my siren dance.

CS: I was in awe of you. I never dreamed we'd ever meet. And now...

ANNA: ...Life throws up many surprises.

CS: D'you know I'm the world's clumsiest man? I daren't ask a woman to dance. Ever. I'm

|||scared I'll tread all over her. Can you teach me?

ANNA: ...I can teach you the steps and rhythm...

CS: (*Jumping to feet*) Can we start now?

ANNA: Which dance d'you have in mind?

CS: The waltz.

ANNA: A good one. Watch me first. (*Anna waltzes with an imaginary partner*) Left right left, right left right. Simple. Now you. (*CS stands, mimics what Anna has just done*) Good. Now with me. Ready? Left right left, right left right. And again? Left... right... left... no right... left... yes... yes...

CS dances the waltz not very well

Dance comes to an end. They stand awkwardly holding each other

CS lightly kisses Anna on cheek. She does not respond

ANNA: I have to go.

CS: Already?

ANNA: I have to see Mother before lights out. Make sure she's comfy.

CS: About your mother... I may be able to help...

ANNA: I would see that as an act of true kindness.

CS: I have some influence. I'm subject to orders myself of course but I can sometimes tweak things.

ANNA: If you could my life would be worth something again. I could look forward to

	things. I'm sure my dancing would get ten times better.
CS:	We can have longer together next time. If I can plan it. (*Change of tone*) So you've dusted, swept and polished?
ANNA:	Well... I don't think I...
CS:	That's the story everyone must hear.
ANNA:	Yes.
CS:	...I'm sure I can do something for your mother...
ANNA:	Can I change? (*Indicates her dance dress*)
CS:	Of course. Please...

Anna walks into the next room through the door. CS sits. Sips whisky

CS:	Thanks for the lesson.
ANNA:	(*Off, behind door*) I love to teach dance...
CS:	A pure moment in a dull day.

CS opens drawer, takes a thin gold ring out

ANNA:	(*Off*) Dance lights up the world...
CS:	Something my mother says. 'It's easy to add to the world's misery Conrad - it's harder to cheer people up.'

Anna re-enters room

She is now back in her everyday clothes, carrying dance dress in a cotton bag

ANNA:	That's a lovely thing to say.
CS:	Who knows, maybe one day you two can meet...
ANNA:	When the world's back to normal.
CS:	Anna I'd like to give you this. (*CS hands her the ring*)
ANNA:	(*Looks*) It's lovely.
CS:	Take it.
ANNA:	I can't. (*She nods no*)
CS:	Why not?
ANNA:	People will want to know where it came from.
CS:	Can't you hide it?
ANNA:	(*Inspecting it*) Where *did* it come from?
CS:	I bought it for someone very... Well... it was given back. Take it. Please. A mark of my appreciation.
ANNA:	If I could keep it hidden...
CS:	So you will?
ANNA:	Yes... (*Puts it carefully in a pocket that buttons*)
CS:	Thank you. Can you wait for me in the car? I won't be a moment...

Anna smiles, exits

CS goes to phone. Dials. Waits. Someone answers

CS:	Pearl, CS here. Take a Mrs Ette Hilmann off the list for next Tuesday. Give 'too ill to be

moved at present time'. Do it now. Make sure Victor Gerrin the news. If he asks if I'm behind it just smile.

Replaces phone. Exits

Lights down

END OF SCENE 4

SCENE FIVE

Two hours after previous scene. Darkening evening

Peter and Anna together

They walk in an open area within perimeter fence

They halt on rough ground, muddy gone hard

They sit but somewhat apart, not speaking

PETER: ...Anna tell me.

ANNA: ...There's nothing to tell.

PETER: You went out of the Centre in his car to his house.

ANNA: His house is outside the Centre. I can't dust and clean it if I don't go to it.

PETER: You danced for him.

ANNA: For us. Above all for my mum. She's in a bad situation or had you forgotten?

PETER: Did he touch you?

ANNA: Don't cross-question me.

PETER: Then answer my question.

ANNA: ...I was teaching him to waltz. You can't teach someone to waltz without holding them.

PETER: Is that all – holding?

ANNA: Yes.

PETER: No kissing, no fondling...?

ANNA: No.

PETER: I'll kill him if he so much as...

ANNA: ...He didn't.

PETER: When I think of you with him I want to cut his arms off.

ANNA: That'd be a challenge – teaching an armless man to dance.

PETER: Are you seeing him again?

ANNA: I'm his cleaning woman Peter. It's weekly. I can't just stop.

PETER: You can if you want.

ANNA: We agreed on a plan.

PETER: Not me.

ANNA: The rest of us then. Can't you support me? It would make it so much easier if you did.

PETER: Not if it means you being alone with him.

ANNA: D'you think you're the only one of us who has feelings?

PETER: He's not a nice man. He signs off everything that happens here. You can't tell me that makes him good to be with.

ANNA: He's a means to an end.

PETER: An upsetting means.

ANNA: I have to keep my mother here. I can't think of any other way.

PETER: You really think if CS fancies you your mother can be saved?

ANNA: I want him to like my dancing not fancy me.

PETER: And I was born yesterday.

ANNA: ...He's not such a monster.

PETER: There are two views on that.

ANNA: At least he doesn't beat us, like they beat you in Amersfoort.

PETER: Hah. Believe it or not that had a good side.

ANNA: Being beaten half to death?

PETER: Being sent straight to hospital here. It meant I got to see you. When you visited. I waited for you every day. I pined. The first time you smiled at me I was head in the stars.

ANNA: I wondered who this injured man was who sat on his bed and stared at me like a ninny. One day I said hallo. To see if you'd dive under the blanket.

PETER: I said hallo back. There was no holding us... we chatted about everything.

ANNA: Was I married? Did I have a boyfriend?

PETER: You said no to both. Are you ever head in the stars when you see me Anna?

ANNA: You're very precious to me.

PETER: Is that as good?

ANNA: As precious as Mother and Millie.

PETER: That's not the sort of precious I want to be.

ANNA: It's as precious as anyone can be.

Peter kisses Anna passionately. Anna quiet

PETER: Love me like I love you.

ANNA: How can people love in here?

PETER: People can love anywhere. (*Anna silent*) Alright don't. As long as I can hug and kiss you.

Anna kisses Peter

ANNA: Our freedom can't be far away. The allies are winning. I pray they win soon so we can be who we really are.

PETER: Don't pray. Act.

ANNA: I do both.

PETER: (*Looks hard at Anna*) Does Schaffer leave things lying round? Papers... letters...? Can you keep an eye out?

ANNA: Yes.

PETER: One paper is all we need. To unlock the secret of the transports.

ANNA: I'll do my best.

PETER: If you find something, memorise it. Don't take it.

ANNA: Okay.

Enter Victor

VICTOR: ...Found you at last you little hideaways. Anna Hosanna – luckiest girl on earth - prepare yourself for good news. Your mother is saved.

ANNA: Saved?

VICTOR: Her name's off the list. She's not going. No less a man than Pearl sought me out to tell me.

ANNA: That's such... I'm... this is silly... (*Close to tears*) ...I must tell Mother and Millie. Thank you... thank you Victor. (*Anna hugs Victor. Tearful*)

Anna exits

VICTOR: What d'you say now Mr Sceptic? A loved one off the list? You can't argue with that.

PETER: Just make sure you don't sacrifice a brave woman for a short-term gain is what I can say, Mr Machiavel.

VICTOR: Don't be so apocalyptic. When you've won a victory, enjoy it.

PETER: We need to organise the residents for a mass breakout not play dangerous games with CS.

VICTOR: Can I remind you – if *one* person tries to escape from here their family's on a transport within a week. Imagine if a lot of us tried.

PETER: Ever the optimist Victor?

VICTOR: Ever the realist Peter. Talking of real, have you written the song for Millie you've been promising me for I don't know how long?

PETER: Yes.

VICTOR: My god. Title?

PETER: 'My Horrible Boss'

VICTOR: Who knows – I may like it despite its title. Lyrics my friend.

PETER: (*Sing song chant*) My horrible boss works me till I'm half insane
Breaking up pieces of the aeroplane.
I do my work and I do it awful quick
'Cause I'm doing it to music do you dig...?'

VICTOR: Stop. I've heard enough. Where's the romance?

PETER: It's a satire. On the work we do. It's not meant to be romantic.

VICTOR: Balls to satire. We've got a young audience - they want songs about passion... love...

Peter in a sing song chant again

PETER: 'I tell it to the stars so bright in the sky that I love you
I say it to the daisies with a great big sigh that I love you
There's only one boy who can make my heart fry
It is you, it is you, only yoo-oo.

VICTOR: That's perfect.

PETER: It maintains that high level of drivel through all three verses.

VICTOR: The youth will love it.

PETER: And my 'Horrible Boss' number?

VICTOR: Back-pocket. The 'I-love-you' song is good. Millie'll sing it in her most arch and innocent way. You'll have a hit and my show will get praised. Time to rehearse my friend.

END OF SCENE 5

SCENE SIX

Hospital ward – Ette's bed

A bit later

Millie spoons liquid into Ette's mouth

ETTE: (*Grimacing*) Nurse, she's torturing me. I may not live another five minutes. I hate, loathe and detest beetroot. It gives me allergies.

MILLIE: Because you fill yourself up with so much rubbish your body can't deal with healthy food.

ETTE: Doctor help, my daughter's poisoning me. She wants to turn my insides blood-red.

MILLIE: Mum shush. Stop acting like a child.

ETTE: I can't stand beetroot.

MILLIE: Alright. Leave it. Be unhealthy. Why should I care?

ETTE: I'm saved. God be praised.

MILLIE: Will you at least lie down?

ETTE: Why? What now?

MILLIE: Your eye. I want to put a crystal on it. (*Millie shows mother a turqoise crystal*)

ETTE: A stone you mean? What good will that do?

MILLIE: Help to heal it.

ETTE: How?

MILLIE: ...Beneficial forces. (*Ette snorts*) Yes Mum. It helped me when my eyes were sore.

ETTE: I thought the doctor's ointment did.

MILLIE: ...Both. They act together. But for now we don't have ointment. So lie down and close your eyes.

Ette manouevres herself down on bed with a few groans. Millie places a jet black stone on one of Ette's eye-lids

ETTE: You and your stones...

MILLIE: Ssh. Keep the eye shut. Think good thoughts. Think better eye.

Enter Anna

ANNA: Mum, Millie I've got the best news ever. (*Millie helps Ette into sitting position on bed*) Are you ready?

ETTE: If it's good news I want to be sitting up. (*Sits up Millie's crystal falls on floor*)

ANNA: Your name's been taken off the list. You're free to stay.

MILLIE: Happiness. I'll cry. (*Millie hugs her mother. She hugs Anna. She's in tears*) I'm such a softie...

ANNA: I checked with Pearl. He confirmed it.

Millie searches for crystal under bed

ETTE: Did he say why?

ANNA: Why...? Well I... he wouldn't tell me would he.

ETTE: Pearl's worse than a snake. How would you ever trust what he says?

ANNA: Snake or not he was clear. You're staying.

ETTE: And this is your wonderful news?

ANNA: Best news I said.

ETTE: It's not best for your father. If I'm not going there's zero chance of me finding him.

MILLIE: Mum's right. Poor Dad but we have to take things a step at a time. (*Finds stone*) Found it! Phew.

ETTE: I know what he'll be doing... he'll be sitting on a chair, in a world of his own, neglecting himself...

ANNA: ...On that chair on his own neglecting himself... no chance of us forgetting that.

MILLIE: And we don't want to forget it do we Anna? I can't tell you how much I... we miss Dad. So we can only imagine how much you miss him. You were so close.

ETTE: A man like your father – an intellectual man, a university lecturer, mind teeming with numbers and stuff – needs a practical person like me to look after him.

MILLIE: Yes Mum, we agree with everything you say about Dad don't we Anna?

ANNA: Christ sake Mother, d'you want us to go back to Pearl and demand your name be put back on?

ETTE: What's so funny about that?

ANNA:	Nothing. We're not laughing. Can't you be sensible for a change? That journey will be a trial for you in your state of health and there's no guarantee you'll find father at the end of it.
ETTE:	Well... let it rest. None of us will be here for much longer anyway.
MILLIE:	Why'd'you say that Mum? Has someone told you something?
ETTE:	A feeling. What d'your stones say Millie? Don't they have the answers?
MILLIE:	They say will Ette Hilmann stop feeling sorry for herself and appreciate what her daughters are doing for her. (*Ette fidgets on her bed*)
ANNA:	Like bringing you this apple for example.

Anna hands Ette withered apple

ETTE:	The second attempt on my life today. Your sister tries to kill me with beetroot juice, now you want to do it with apple. Apple blocks up my throat.
ANNA:	I'll bite bits off and chew them. Then you can swallow.
ETTE:	One piece.
ANNA:	The whole lot. (*Anna bites off small piece, chews it. Hands it to Ette who takes piece and eats it*) Well? How is it?
ETTE:	As nice as chewed apple can be.

Anna bites off second small piece, chews it, hands it to Ette who eats. Anna repeats this five or six times

	You and Millie eat the rest?
MILLIE:	We've already eaten. Well I have.
ETTE:	Go on. To please your poor mother?
ANNA:	Mum you're so stubborn.
ETTE:	Give me a tiny bit of pleasure?

Anna and Millie share half the apple. Anna gives Ette another piece she's chewed. Ette eats it

	(*To Anna*) How was it got off?
ANNA:	What?
ETTE:	My name? And at the last minute?
ANNA:	You can thank our hard work. Millie and I haven't stopped Mum. We've talked to every important person in the Centre.
MILLIE:	Talked *at* every important person you mean.
ANNA:	Quite. We said a long journey would... well... would...
ETTE:	...Kill me?
ANNA:	...I don't know we said kill you...
MILLIE:	I did. Sorry wasn't I meant to?
ANNA:	...Be very bad for you anyway. In your present state of health.
MILLIE:	'Specially if you ended up dying.
ETTE:	Who were these important persons you spoke to?
ANNA:	(*Guarded*) ...Pearl.

ETTE:	He doesn't listen to anyone unless there's a bribe.
MILLIE:	I spoke to Dr Starmer. He's very important.
ANNA:	Mishen.
ETTE:	So those warm-hearted men took my name off the list because they didn't want to see a poor old lady suffer?
MILLIE:	We touched their hearts Mum. We know the art of persuasion.
ETTE:	There are people in here iller than me. Their names are still on.
ANNA:	Yes well maybe Millie and I have more influence than they do.
MILLIE:	...Because we're artistes. So many people know us. I get asked for my autograph everywhere... specially in the canteen when I'm queuing.
ETTE:	How come you knew first Anna?
ANNA:	Well I... I bumped into Pearl.
ETTE:	You said you checked with Pearl. You either bump into someone or you check with them.
ANNA:	Did I say 'check'?
ETTE:	Yes.
ANNA:	...I've been going to Pearl all the time to check.
ETTE:	It's not what you said.
ANNA:	Well I meant to.

MILLIE: It could just as easily have been me if I'd been to check...

ETTE: Own up – what was the bargain?

ANNA: What are you talking about? What bargain?

ETTE: The one you struck to get my name off. It's the only way things happen in here...

ANNA: We just simply talked...

MILLIE: But to important people. We know all of them don't we Anna. They regard us so highly.

ETTE: You're hiding something. Come on tell – what did you offer?

ANNA: We haven't got anything *to* offer... unless you want Millie to offer her crystals?

ETTE: An attractive young woman has always got something she can offer.

ANNA: A beautiful young woman has... what? I hope you're not insinuating what I think you are...?

MILLIE: Mum you're being very rude...

ANNA: Are you suggesting we offered ourselves? Is that the 'something' you mean?

ETTE: I'm trying to find out that's all.

ANNA: That's horrible. That you could think such a thing of your own daughters.

ETTE: Oh don't get on your high horse with me.

ANNA: I'll get on it and gallop all over you if you dare say such a thing again.

ETTE: I didn't say it.

ANNA: You implied it.

MILLIE: Please calm down will you both please? Come on... Mum, Anna, deep breaths... for me...

ANNA: I'll calm down when she apologises.

MILLIE: Oh Anna aren't we stupid. I can't believe how stupid we've been. How could we have forgotten the most important person – the one who helped Mother out more than anyone?

ANNA: (*Worried*) Millie you promised, don't you dare...

MILLIE: Victor Gerrin of course.

ANNA: Oh Victor. Yes Victor. He made all the difference. He spoke to Pearl and Mishen about you Mother.

MILLIE: We hear he even spoke to Schaffer.

ANNA: Victor can do that. He's a favourite of his. Yes Victor swung it in your favour. Fancy forgetting that.

ETTE: Well why didn't you tell me when I asked? Letting me think of bargains women can make to get their way.

ANNA: We were pigmies compared to the famous Victor Gerrin. His help clinched it not any 'something' we had to offer.

MILLIE: Mother doesn't think we did do that now do you Mother?

ETTE:	Not now you've explained. Oh this place – it makes you think the worst of everyone when there are so many good people in here. Please forgive me, darling daughters. You want the best for me. I love you dearly. Thank you for your help. Thank you for your concern. Now that's enough excitement for today. Dream-time calls. I need to sleep. It's my favourite time – dreaming of the past. Dad and I in the park, you two skipping around... Can you leave me now?
ANNA:	Happy dream-time Mother.
ETTE:	It's calling me. Bye my lovely daughters. Thanks for thinking of me. I'm glad I'm staying with you though sad your father's still alone. I'll go to sleep and dream I can write him a letter that he can read. I'll give him all our news.
ANNA:	We'll see you tomorrow.
ETTE:	Yes now go.
MILLIE:	Night then. Goodnight. Sweet dreams.

Exit Millie and Anna

Lights down

END OF SCENE 6

SCENE SEVEN

CS's living room, late afternoon

A few days later

Anna dusts alone

She looks in various drawers. Finds some papers in one. Takes them out, reads through them quickly

Front door opens, closes off

Anna hurriedly puts papers back, shuts drawer, continues dusting as CS enters

CS: Hallo Anna. Mm... the house looks spotless. You've been working hard.

ANNA: I've kept a steady pace.

CS walks to chest of drawers. He finds cigarettes and a cigarette-lighter. Lights himself a cigarette

CS: Could you fetch me a glass of water please Anna?

He hands Anna an empty glass

Anna exits SR to kitchen with glass

CS looks in drawer anna just looked in. He carefully takes out papers Anna has just looked at, studies them, puts them in jacket pocket. Waits

Anna returns and hands him a glass of water

CS: Today I'd like a song. Can you sing for me?

ANNA: I haven't sung for ages.

CS: But you can sing?

ANNA: I always sang before I handed singing-duties to my sister...

CS: So you will?

MILLIE: A sad or a happy song?

CS: Sad.

ANNA: Forgive me if I don't reach the heights.

CS: Please.

ANNA: (*Sings*) Your heart is full of longing
But disappointment too,
Tears and laughter
And that's called love.

It's there when you say adieu,
When you try to forget
There when you long to have him back.

It gives you times
You really can't forget.
Makes you crave a heart
And want it close to you,
So that once you find it
You'll never let it go.
Yes love true love is a mystery

CS: (*After a while*) ...A lovely song.

ANNA: The only one I can remember.

CS: Sit down please. (*Anna sits. CS pours himself second whisky*) Can I talk to you? In confidence?

ANNA: Of course.

CS: I feel trapped. Every little thing in this Centre depends on me. I'm the axis, the turning point. If I took a day off the place would grind to a halt. Of course the residents don't think of that. All they think about is themselves, as if no one else had problems. I don't blame them. I'd be the same in their position. But I'm not. They are my work. Every waking moment is filled up by them. I'm the shepherd, they're my flock. Them and everything to do with them. Yes trapped is a good word. And no way out till the chaos ends. (*Anna stares at him*) Thank you for listening. Now can we waltz? I've been practising.

ANNA: I look forward to the results.

CS puts dance music on. Takes Anna in his arms. They waltz. He's better than last time

CS: Well?

ANNA: Good. Much lighter on your feet.

CS holds Anna tighter and tighter

CS: I've dreamed of this. From when I first saw you. Dreamed I'd dance with you...

He kisses her. Then hugs her close – aroused.

Anna forces herself not to resist. CS puts his body close up against Anna's. He's 'intimate' with her though fully clothed. It's like a rape

After a while he stops. Walks away from her. Anna re-arranges her clothes

CS: Are you...?

ANNA: Yes...?

CS: ...You didn't stop me...

ANNA: I haven't complained have I?

CS: When a man and a woman dance things like that can happen.

ANNA: I'm here as your teacher.

CS: I've never had such a beautiful one.

ANNA: Beautiful or not, a teacher is a teacher.

CS: I've been an unruly student.

ANNA: Get your discipline back.

CS: Was it unpleasant?

ANNA: That's not a word I'd use.

CS: D'you have any feelings for me Anna?

ANNA: ...As far as they're allowed in here.

CS: If we were in the normal world, would you go out with me? Marry me even?

ANNA: As much as I could any man. I travel all the time... endless travel... it's my life. It's hard to settle down.

CS: Anna are you here because you want to be or because others want you to be?

ANNA: Why would I do what someone else wants?

CS: To help them? Because they see an advantage?

ANNA: I'm here because I want to teach dance and you want to be taught.

CS: Just to teach dance?

ANNA: ...Who I'm teaching... that too.

CS: You're not forcing yourself to be with me?

ANNA: No. Why'd'you ask?

CS: Why did you look through my papers?

ANNA: (*Startled*) Sorry? Why did I...?

CS: ...My private papers? A trick I play. (*He takes out the papers from pocket*) I place a hair here. On the surface. (*He shows Anna where hair was placed*) If it moves I know someone's touched them.

ANNA: No I... had to pull... to dust. It wouldn't come... then it came with a whoosh! (*Mimics movement*)

CS: The hair's gone. Vanished.

ANNA: I pulled the drawer, that's all I did.

CS: If I thought you'd gone through my papers I'd wonder if you were here because you enjoyed my company or because someone'd set you up to spy on me. Gerrin say. Or Peter the comedian.

ANNA: The drawer jumped. That's all I can say.

CS: (*Awkward moment*) I loved the song. It washed over me. I'm refreshed. (*Awkward moment*) Well, shall we...? (*He indicates the door*)

ANNA: ...My mother... We owe it to you.

CS: (*Stands*) Thank you for the song. You sang it beautifully. I'll remember it for a long time to come.

CS shakes hands with her. Anna disconcerted, finds this gesture out of the normal

> I'm looking forward to the show tomorrow. I've invited lots of friends. Gerrin won't let me down I know...

Anna exits, CS behind her

Sound fx off: front door opens, closes. Car door opens, closes

Lights down

END OF SCENE 7

SCENE EIGHT

Small room off large hall

Later same day, evening

Bits and pieces of stage scenery propped against walls

Sound of small band rehearsing from adjoining hall

Victor runs through his master of ceremonies lines

VICTOR: ...Good evening to you and you... but not to you. Because you laugh in the wrong places that's why.

Enter Peter in suit shirt, tie – smart

PETER: ...Have you seen Anna?

VICTOR: Not yet.

PETER: She should've been back ages ago.

VICTOR: (*Back to sketch*) ...When I told you to stop laughing last time you know what you said? My lazy eye set you off. (*He mimics this*) Let me tell you young man, nothing about me's lazy. Daft maybe. Slow on the uptake. Lazy never... (*Now speaks lines to himself*)

PETER: What's keeping her?

VICTOR: My sketches are so old they're decrepit.

PETER: She should be here.

VICTOR: (*To Peter*) I've got a knack for making the old seem new but my repertoire's so old it's rancid.

Peter looks at door, worrying about Anna

PETER: ...What?

VICTOR: Sketch? Me? In need of?

PETER: Sketch...?

VICTOR: New one? Funny one? For me? Be democratic and share – that's your philosophy isn't it Peter?

PETER: How about this? A Jew arrives at a holiday-*camp*...

VICTOR: ...Holiday-camp you say?

PETER: Picture it. The searching first questions. 'What's your name?' 'How old are you?' 'Are you a man or a woman?' Questions that test your mental powers to the limit.

VICTOR: Oh oh, I see where this is leading. CS isn't going to like it.

PETER: Where's his sense of humour?

VICTOR: He likes innocent stuff.

PETER: Custard pies and bare thighs?

VICTOR: Where's the harm? If it makes people laugh?

PETER: The fact that's all it does?

VICTOR: Laughter lifts the spirits. Bare thighs lift something else. Both precious.

Enter Millie in alpine-maid country-girl costume – long dress, short puff sleeves, button-up collar, blue gingham

MILLIE: Look at this dress. I love it! When I wear a dress like this I sing better.

PETER: Only Jewish songs my little Jew warbler.

MILLIE: They're the best. Ask me nicely I'll sing some for you.

PETER: I certainly will...

MILLIE: I hope you to mean that.

PETER: Have you seen Anna?

MILLIE: Why're you always thinking about Anna when you talk to me?

PETER: Have you seen her?

MILLIE: Not since she went off to clean.

PETER: That was ages ago.

MILLIE: You don't ask about me when I'm not here do you Peter?

PETER: Do... if the show's about to start...

MILLIE: (*Mock sigh*) If only that were true... (*To Victor*) I've chosen my opening number Victor. 'The Little Girl with the Innocent Air'.

VICTOR: Slot three plus slot eight with 'Oh how Often'.

MILLIE: Only two for poor ickle me?

VICTOR: For now...

MILLIE: But I must sing 'I'm a Woman Who Knows What She Wants'.

VICTOR: Keep it for in case.

PETER: ...In case we lose a performer at the last minute?

MILLIE: (*To Victor*) ...Let me squeeze it in?

VICTOR: I've got ten artists for the show and they all want to squeeze something in.

MILLIE: But I'm your favourite.

VICTOR: You will be if you let *me* squeeze something in.

MILLIE: Ugh! You're much too old. I'd feel like I was making love to my father.

VICTOR: To a father-figure you mean little duckling...

MILLIE: Grandfather even. It makes me shudder thinking about it. Change the subject.

VICTOR: You started this conversation.

MILLIE: You took it in a suggestive direction.

VICTOR: How'd'you know that?

MILLIE: It's so obvious.

VICTOR: Maybe that reflects the way your mind works.

MILLIE: When someone makes a suggestive remark, I know.

Enter Anna in hurry

VICTOR: Anna, star of the show, we've been worrying about you. Well Peter has. The rest of us have been too busy getting ready.

ANNA: ...Has my dress arrived?

VICTOR: In that bag. (*Points to a large cloth bag*)

Anna unlaces bag. Pulls out white flowing robe, Isadora Duncan style. Holds it up to her body

ANNA: Good.

VICTOR: You can thank you-know-who for it.

ANNA: I thank you-know-who for a lot of things.

MILLIE: Like what for example?

ANNA: Don't ask questions.

MILLIE: I can't help it if you say things that provoke me to.

ANNA: No sorry, I'm sorry. I'm late and I'm not ready, that's all. I didn't mean to snap.

PETER: (*Quiet*) How did your meeting with the lord of darkness go?

MILLIE: Try your dress on Anna. I can't wait to see it on you.

ANNA: Yes yes... I will. I must.

MILLIE: I'm more than pleased with mine. It fits me like a glove. (*She pirouettes*)

ANNA: Yes very elegant, milk-maid you.

VICTOR: We start in five. Anna you're first is the 'Gavotte'...

ANNA: ...And my 'Wicked Witch' dance slot six, yes yes, all rehearsed, all ready.

MILLIE: I need to tell the musicians about my *two* songs.

VICTOR: I need to do a final check so let's go together. Hurry up Anna – the hall's filling up.

Exit Victor and Millie

Anna changes into costume

PETER: Did you dust to standard?

ANNA: I dusted.

PETER: Did you dance?

ANNA: No. (*Taking work clothes off & putting dance-dress on*)

PETER: Why not?

ANNA: He wanted me to sing.

PETER: To sing? Well well... and did you?

ANNA: Yes.

PETER: What did you sing?

ANNA: 'Love Is a Mystery'.

PETER: Whose choice was that?

ANNA: He wanted a sad song. It was the only one I... I'm sorry...

PETER: I love that song. It's one of my best.

ANNA: It moved him.

PETER: Would he have been moved if he'd known who wrote it? And who it was for? (*Looks straight at Anna*)

ANNA: I did what you asked. Searched his house. He'd left some papers in a drawer. I read as much of them as I could.

PETER: What were they about?

ANNA: ...Furniture. Probably someone else's.

Anna is now in her dance costume

PETER: Desperate for facts about what waits us at the end of that journey we turn up an order for tables and chairs.

ANNA: I'm sorry...

PETER: ...I bet he burns important stuff. Or doesn't put it in writing. Leave no proof.

ANNA: I think he knew I'd looked.

PETER: You didn't take them?

ANNA: (*Nods no*) He'd laid a hair on them. He said it had moved.

PETER: Cunning bastard.

ANNA: ...The drawer jumped I said...

PETER: ...He makes such a thing of his high standards then behaves like that.

ANNA: ...Was I with him because I liked him or because someone saw an advantage...? (*Peter and Anna reflect*)

PETER: Someone...?

ANNA: Victor. You.

PETER: He named our names?

ANNA: Yes.

PETER: He's hit the truth with Victor.

ANNA: You saw an interest too.

PETER: After I couldn't stop you meeting him. Only then.

ANNA: I told him I was there because of my love of dance.

Anna goes through a dance warm-up routine from now on

PETER: He could think you're nosy. You're in the house... you're on your own... you see some papers... you have a look.

ANNA: That would be good.

PETER: Or he could think you're using him so you can get into his house to read through his private papers?

ANNA: That would be bad.

PETER: We need him to think you're nosy. You can be nosy and still like him and want to be with him.

ANNA: I think he thinks I was spying...

Enter Victor followed by Millie

VICTOR: ...We're sold out my chickens. Another full house.

MILLIE: CS is there, surrounded by his gleaming SS guests.

PETER: Come to see his performing pets. Can I use a gun in my act?

VICTOR: Only if it shoots flags.

Anna has been limbering up for some time. Millie does some voice warm-up exercises

Are we ready Anna?

ANNA: Yes.

MILLIE: Me too.

VICTOR: Peter?

PETER: As I'll ever be.

Victor makes questioning sign to other side of stage then a thumbs up

VICTOR: Then let the show begin.

Victor walks on to the stage

(*Off*) Ladies and gentlemen... oh and you... and even you sir. Welcome to tonight's fabulous mix of laughter mirth and mayhem. (*Laughter off*). We're especially honoured tonight by the presence of our esteemed and treasured leader and his noble guests... and I don't include the man there in the third row yes you sir with the smirk and the huge tidemark on your neck – honestly some people. No I mean none other than the director of our wonderful Centre, the encourager of cultural and educational activities, our very esteemed beloved Commandant...

PETER: (*Quietly*) God how Victor crawls.

ANNA: If he does we don't have to so be thankful.

VICTOR: (*Off*) ...Tonight's treasure of song, dance and comedy is called 'The World's Gone Mad'. So without more ado on with our opening sketch - 'How to hang a man without wasting rope'...

Lights fade to black

END OF SCENE 8

SCENE NINE

THE SHOW

The following acts take place on stage

Peter & Victor act out a comedy sketch (mime based): in a restaurant. A guest complains about his food so much the waiter ends up hanging himself by his tie but somehow escaping death

Anna dances solo – 'la gavotte' – flirtatious and humorous but underlying tension or waitress nearly spilling tray of drinks or young woman comically learning to ice-skate

Millie sings 'the little girl with the innocent air'

Thunderous applause

Lights fade

END OF SCENE 9

SCENE 10

Some days later, sunday, late afternoon

Scrubby open ground inside perimeter fence. Some scruffy bedraggled bushes

Peter and anna wrapped in layers of thin clothing against chill wind. They huddle together

ANNA: ...How I'd love to get away – even for a few hours. Walk down the streets where I was born. Catch a tram to the arcade. Look in shop windows.

PETER: I feel the same.

ANNA: I've got an escape-plan...

PETER: You'd need one of those.

ANNA: It's meal-time – inmates and guards all focused on food. I approach the camp-gates, you a safe distance behind. I offer the guards a cheese I've saved from my food-parcel. It's very smelly. They open the gate. I shove the cheese under their noses. The moment they breathe it in, they pass out. Hand in hand we walk out to freedom.

PETER: (*Laughing*) What then?

ANNA: We find a barn. We cuddle up.

PETER: Live on beetroots and berries?

ANNA: Whatever we can lay our hands on.

PETER: And drink?

ANNA: We milk a passing cow.

PETER: Why didn't I think of this?

ANNA: We hide in the day and move at night.

PETER: Move where? The first nosy Dutchman who sees us will report us.

ANNA: The world's asleep.

PETER: The whole world?

ANNA: We hope.

PETER: Then what?

ANNA: We contact the resistance.

PETER: How?

ANNA: As we walk we hold up a sign. 'Help if you're Resistance.' (*They laugh*)

PETER: It'll be dark. No one will see.

ANNA: I've not thought this through have I?

PETER: I've... got a plan myself.

ANNA: I hope it's better than mine.

PETER: We note where the perimeter fence has been weakened. At the right moment, when the guards are dozing, we crawl under it and out. Two bikes are waiting. They're hidden but I know where.

ANNA: How do you?

PETER: A contact on the outside has got word to me. We cycle to a safe house. We hide. Every few days we move and hide, each time in a safe house.

ANNA: How did we find a contact on the outside?

PETER: Through a contact on the inside. The Reception Centre hero. The person in a hundred who works there who'll risk their life to get a message out, get one back and pass it on.

ANNA: Your plan *is* better than mine.

PETER: It's all I think about. I'm not writing songs anymore. I haven't written a letter out in weeks. I don't have noble thoughts about leading a breakout that'll carve my name in the roll-call of resistance heroes. All I think about is how I can get out of this madhouse with its too many people and its wierd routines and its promise of future horrors. I spend my nights dreaming up escape-plans, ready to risk my life...

ANNA: To get away. To walk in a park. Feed the ducks. See old friends...

PETER: Would you take a chance?

ANNA: I'd love to.

PETER: Ready for the challenge?

ANNA: Well I... yes...

PETER: No ifs no buts?

ANNA: Especially if Mother and Millie could come.

PETER: If they couldn't?

ANNA: That would be hard.

PETER: If it could only be me and you?

ANNA: ...I'd worry about them. What would happen to them.

PETER: Put yourself first.

ANNA: ...As if I haven't all my life.

PETER: The Anna I know always puts her mother first.

ANNA: Why am I a dancer? Why did I leave home the minute I signed my first contract? Why aren't I married like Mother thinks I should be and has tried so hard to get me to be? Why have I caused her so much grief?

PETER: That's being independent.

ANNA: It's doing what I want.

PETER: So go on doing it. Don't use your family as an excuse not to.

ANNA: When have I ever done that?

PETER: Now. With your mother. From what you tell me she *wants* to go East. For her it's not a punishment - it's a release.

ANNA: ...Because nothing matters to her except finding Dad. It makes her ignore reality.

PETER: If it's what she wants who are we to say she's wrong?

ANNA: We're people who can help her see what she won't at the moment see.

PETER: Is it right to do that?

ANNA: If it means she stays.

PETER:	So many ifs. There's none with my plan. You check every detail a hundred times then you check them some more. You choose your time. You make your move. You succeed or you fail.
ANNA:	*If* all goes according to plan you succeed. *If* you have bad luck you fail. Two ifs already.
PETER:	Will you come Anna?
ANNA:	What about Millie? What can you say that'll make what will happen to her okay?
PETER:	We pray Lady Luck looks after her through whatever this mad world throws at her.
ANNA:	...I'll be thinking ever after, you did that, put your mother and sister on that train...
PETER:	...All of us will be on that train sooner or later. What difference does a week or two make?
ANNA:	Every week we stay here's a week nearer freedom. We can see the sky light up over Droghten from the nightly bombing raids. We can feel the earth shake. Liberation is getting nearer.
PETER:	And if you're not around to enjoy it?
ANNA:	I hope I will be. *We* will be.
PETER:	That may be a fragile hope.
ANNA:	A growing hope.
PETER:	Not an illusion?
ANNA:	...I don't think death's certain - even at the end of the transport. They'll make us work for

	them in some huge camp. Auschwitz or Sobibor... Theresienstadt. Our usefulness will save us.
PETER:	The rumours of Jews being worked to death? In their hundreds...?
ANNA:	I don't believe them.
PETER:	Come with me Anna?
ANNA:	Seeing as it's all a fantasy I will.
PETER:	Say it's not? Say it's real? (*Anna troubled*) If you love me you'll say yes.
ANNA:	If I do I'll leave loved-ones behind.
PETER:	That's the choice.
ANNA:	My love for you would mean more than my love for them.
PETER:	Different not more.
ANNA:	Just go Peter.
PETER:	With you?
ANNA:	No.
PETER:	Because you can easily do without me?
ANNA:	I can't.
PETER:	Then why aren't you begging me to stay?
ANNA:	I would if I was selfish. You're part of me, part of my life here. No you must go. You can. You're not tied down. If you've really got a plan follow it. Go with my love.

PETER: If you're not with me I'll go without my love.

ANNA: I'll be with you in spirit – guarding you, hiding you.

PETER: Please come with me Anna.

ANNA: Anyway I'm hopeless at crawling and running. I'd hold you back.

PETER: I'd carry you. And then we'd have bikes.

ANNA: In this dream of yours?

PETER: (*After a bit*) ...Say I did go? What about the people I left behind? We know what happens to the friends and family of people who try to escape.

ANNA: Artistes are an exception to the rules. What happens to others doesn't to them.

PETER: Performers have been sent away on transports.

ANNA: If you have a plan worked out, follow it. Your friends can take care of themselves.

PETER: Are you saying I should go? Even if it causes problems for others?

ANNA: I am. With all my heart.

PETER: Say I ask one last time, 'Will you join me?'

ANNA: ...(*She stands*) I'll say I hope you make it. I'd end up with a 'till-we-meet-again' moment... (*They kiss passionately*)

PETER: Anna if you tell me you love me as much as I love you, I'll stay. My word. I'll stay with a

> warm heart and total happiness... So say it? Will you? Please?

Peter looks at Anna. Waits. Anna says nothing

The silence is broken by Millie calling in the darkening evening

MILLIE: (*Off*) Anna? Anna, are you there?

ANNA: Here Millie. (*Millie sees them. Approaches off*)

Enter Millie

MILLIE: (*Sees them*) Sorry to break in. I can't believe it. I can't I just... (*Millie breaks into tears*)

ANNA: Millie pet. What's wrong?

MILLIE: It's like they're playing with us...

ANNA: Why? What is it?

MILLIE: Mum's name. It's back on...

ANNA: Back on what?

MILLIE: The list. Her name is on the list.

ANNA: Not possible.

MILLIE: It is Anna don't tell me it isn't. I've checked.

ANNA: Who told you?

MILLIE: Mum did.

ANNA: (*Relieved*) Oh don't listen to her. She always gets things wrong.

MILLIE: I've just been with her. Horrible Pearl came into the hospital block she said. Into her ward. He called out her name. For next Tuesday.

ANNA:	Maybe she muddled up another name with hers? She's done that before.
MILLIE:	I asked her a hundred times. What's worse – she's happy.
PETER:	Wasn't Victor's plan meant to stop this happening?
ANNA:	We need to check again. If it's true, we just have to do what we did before only a hundred times more strongly.
MILLIE:	Who shall I start with? I need to do something... to keep busy
ANNA:	You try Mishen. I'll speak to Mother...
MILLIE:	I'll find him now.
ANNA:	If she convinces me, I'll see Pearl... and others...
MILLIE:	There's never any calm here. Just when you think things are fine, bang disaster strikes.
ANNA:	Meet by Mum's bed in an hour?
MILLIE:	(*Exiting*) One hour.

Exit Millie at a run

PETER:	That's unwelcome.
ANNA:	Why has it happened...?
PETER:	Couldn't be to do with...?
ANNA:	I hope not.
PETER:	If I thought what I'd asked you to do would lead to any harm...

ANNA: You did what you thought was right. It *was* right. I'll try and find out if the two are connected. (*Change. Quiet voice*) If you're going, go soon. Don't tell me when. Let me find out with everyone else. Be lucky. Don't take chances. Outwit them.

PETER: Let's go together Anna please? (*Anna and Peter kiss*)

ANNA: May the SS and their helpers sleep for a week while you find a safe house. May some kind god muddle their brains so their searches lead to nothing. (*She takes the ring CS gave her from a pocket*) Take this. Use it as barter. (*Puts it on Peter's little finger*) See you after the War. I love you.

PETER: Like a brother?

ANNA: That's the strongest love there is.

Exit Anna

END OF SCENE 10

SCENE ELEVEN

Thirty minutes after previous scene

Main Hall

CS at desk in hall where cabaret takes place, hard at work

Enter Anna. She walks to desk, stands, waits

CS goes on working, does not look up

ANNA: I'll be quick.

CS looks up, sees Anna. He looks around to check no one is in earshot

CS: Anna. This is a surprise.

ANNA: ...It's about my Mother. Two days ago I asked if you'd help get her name off the list. Next day it was. I was so grateful. I had a smile on my face right through the day. Good deeds can happen no matter how difficult the situation I thought. Now her name's back on.

CS: Have you spoken to Pearl?

ANNA: He's too busy. His secretary confirmed Mother was down to leave.

CS: I'll look into it.

ANNA: Is it a punishment?

CS: Sorry? For what?

ANNA: Please tell me. If I've done something wrong I'd like to put it right.

CS: You've done nothing wrong. Your house-cleaning is...

ANNA: Didn't I show enough feeling? When we kissed? When you were being an unruly student? I'm sorry, I felt out of sorts. I had a cold.

CS: You think your mother's on the list because of how we kissed?

ANNA: Yes. No. I don't know. Next time we kiss I'll do better.

CS: You will or you'll pretend to?

ANNA: I *will*. You'll feel it.

CS: This Centre's a poor place for feelings Anna. They don't grow naturally. How would I know what you were feeling when you kissed me?

ANNA: When *you* kissed *me*. That's how I remember it.

CS: You're right. When I kissed you. How did you feel when I kissed you?

ANNA: You should know. From the kiss.

CS stands. Walks round desk, stands near to Anna

CS: Will you be honest with me Anna?

ANNA: I always try to be.

CS: ...Who suggested you got closer to me?

ANNA: I thought it came from you.

CS: Me? Well I...

ANNA: Didn't you ask to meet me in private? After you saw me on stage?

CS: ...I never hid how much I loved your act... I'm still sure someone you know encouraged this.

ANNA: You mean apart from me?

CS: Someone who saw me gawping when you danced? Knew how taken I was with you?

ANNA: Why would I pay attention to someone else?

CS: Perhaps they pointed out what you could gain from it?

ANNA: D'you think that's the reason I danced for you? For what I could get out of it?

CS: Would it be the worst thing in the world?

ANNA: Not if you think prostituting your art's okay.

CS: How is selling your talent at a price it merits prostitution? Especially if it keeps the people you love here?

ANNA: (*Fishing*) Is there a particular reason I should want to keep the people I love here?

CS: Who wants to be separated from their mother?

ANNA: Separation's not as bad as death is it... unless you've got reason to think it is?

CS: It's natural to want to be with loved ones. 'Specially now.

ANNA: What's so special about now?

CS: Questions questions. Every time I say something you fire a question at me.

ANNA: I want to understand what you mean.

CS: So many people arriving, people leaving. Wouldn't you give a lot to be protected from that?

ANNA: The reasons you give for why I might sell my talent make sense only I didn't. Give me more reasons I'll say the same. When I agreed to dance for you it was because of my love of dance.

CS: The same answer as before? Not because you liked me?

ANNA: This place is strange for liking people...

CS: I know I like you.

ANNA: Like what about me? My body? What you can do to it? Like a prisoner in your power you can have any time you want because she's helpless?

CS: ...As the magical woman I've dreamed about ever since I saw you on stage.

ANNA: That's... I... yes... yes...

CS: Be honest with me. I need you to be honest more than ever. Did you open that drawer and look through my papers?

ANNA: ...Yes.

CS: Why? What were you looking for?

ANNA: Answers.

CS: To what?

ANNA: Questions that scratch away at our peace of mind and drive us mad. A thousand Jews leave here every week. The start of a better life we're told. So why's no one eager to go? Why aren't Pearl and Mishen trampling the rest of us underfoot to get to the front of the queue?

CS: You think the answer's in my sideboard?

ANNA: ...I was hoping.

CS: If you're looking for the truth there, you must think I know it. Which means you must think I haven't told you what I know.

ANNA: You have if you only know as much as me.

CS: It's true I haven't pushed myself to find out every detail of what every person is doing in every labour camp in the Reich. I've got my job and it's a lot of work. I can't do it if I don't shut things out that aren't in my sphere.

ANNA: When a person's worried, telling them what you know doesn't help if what you know isn't much more than they do.

CS: Why d'you doubt what I've told you Anna?

ANNA: You can afford to have vague ideas – or no ideas – about what happens in the East. You're not going. But we are. And when we're told we're off to the land of milk and honey but every Tuesday we see people forced into the trucks...

CS: It's forbidden to watch embarcations.

ANNA:	...When no one gets the choice and those that object get kicked on how can I believe in a promised land?
CS:	It's normally calm and orderly...
ANNA:	It doesn't match up. That's why I went through your papers, hoping to find answers you tell me you don't have. I'm sorry. In my normal life I wouldn't dream of doing such a thing.
CS:	Someone's put you up to this. It was Peter wasn't it?
ANNA:	No.
CS:	Gerrin then? Devious oily Victor
ANNA:	I decided myself. Why won't you believe me? Aren't I capable of making a decision? Do I always have to have a man behind me, thinking for me?
CS:	(*Takes stock*) ...It upset me, that papers business. You felt nothing for me, you were using me, laughing at me behind my back...
ANNA:	Not true.
CS:	...I think now it's not...
ANNA:	Then are we friends now?
CS:	...I was so angry I couldn't sleep that night. That a woman I felt so much for could treat me like that, like a fool...
ANNA:	But I didn't.

CS: ...When I'm in that mood I shouldn't take decisions. How many times have I told myself? 'Don't do anything till you've calmed down Conrad. You'll regret it.' But I never listen...

ANNA: Did you then? Take a decision...?

CS: A petty one.

ANNA: What I did with your papers wasn't very noble...

CS: I had your mother's name put back on the list. It's nothing, I can change it. But I... well I did something more difficult to... which I wish I hadn't... (*Off on a burst*) You know I have to report spying. Or the suspicion of it. My bosses take it very seriously.

ANNA: (*Dawns*) ...Spying? Who on earth...? (*Realisation*) You don't mean when I...?

CS: (*Awkward silence*) I'll phone HQ. You were doing your job. I'd asked you to dust all surfaces, including drawers. I forgot I had. My mistake. Sorry for the false alarm. No one was spying, matter closed. (*Anna quiet*) It'll be fine. If I make a point of correcting something they always accept.

ANNA: I don't need to worry then...?

CS: You don't. (*CS approaches Anna. Puts her hand to his chest*) Feel my heart... if we're talking about feelings.

ANNA: You said we couldn't know how people feel in here.

CS:	My heartbeat's real.
ANNA:	But what's it beating for?
CS:	It only happens when I'm with you or when I'm thinking about you.
ANNA:	Then keep me and my family here if you like it beating like this. (*Removes her hand from his chest*)
CS:	I've told you what I'm going to do. There won't be a problem.
ANNA:	They'll forget what you said about...?
CS:	No doubt about it. You don't need to worry about that. Now will you clean as usual Wednesday?
ANNA:	If you want me to sing I need to know.
CS:	To dance. I don't want to upset anyone.
ANNA:	Who would it upset?
CS:	I read through my cabaret programmes last night. Who wrote which songs.
ANNA:	The one I sang...?
CS:	I know who wrote it. Better to stick to dance. Safer.
ANNA:	If you hear from your bosses... the spying thing...
CS:	You don't need to worry.
ANNA:	Till Wednesday.

Anna turns, walks out of hall

CS picks up phone

CS: ...HQ please. (*Waits*) Aus der Funten's office. (*Waits*) Conrad Schaffer here sir. I forwarded a report – case of spying? Can it be binned? I've cleared the matter up to my complete satisfaction and... (*Listens*) You have? I see. I know the importance we give to security but I made a mistake. I'd asked my cleaner to dust all surfaces and... Well I just thought... I'm a hundred per cent sure she wasn't spying. (*Interrupted*) They all will in the end sir but I do feel in this... But my suspicions were... No sir, I have no relationship with the woman outside of a professional one. Absolutely not. No. No that was it. Thank you.

CS puts phone down. Unhappy

Lights down

END OF SCENE 11

SCENE 12

Two days later, Monday. Late afternoon

Exterior. Victor, Anna & Millie sit next to a primitive railway platform that cuts through the middle of the camp. They each have a small shoulder bag for a journey

Sfx: many people waiting to board

No Peter

VICTOR: ...Until they bolt the doors you can still get a recall.

MILLIE: I saw Mishen pull a man off a train last week. Grabbed him by the trouser-leg and yanked him off. (*She mimics action*) Bumpity bumpity bump.

VICTOR: A blood-line problem most likely. A hundred years ago a Jew married an Aryan which begat a half Jew who then married an Aryan which begat a quarter Jew and blah and blee...

MILLIE: I don't mind what sort of Jew I'm next to as long as he's fit and handsome.

VICTOR: I'd love to oblige Millie but Mishen'll have that deferral in my sweaty little mitt any time now.

MILLIE: Today could be the only time in my life I wish I had Aryan blood in me.

VICTOR: That can be taken in more senses than one Millie.

MILLIE: Only by people with minds like yours Victor.

ANNA: The only person I know who has Aryan blood is Peter. He's got two German grandparents... one on each side...

VICTOR: ...Don't mention that man's name in front of me. He can burn in hell fire forever and it wouldn't be good enough for him.

ANNA: Victor that's horrible.

VICTOR: Is there a reason it shouldn't be?

ANNA: He's your friend...?

VICTOR: My closest. I loved Peter. (*Sign*) We were like that. Like father and son - always quarrelling, always laughing...

ANNA: So remember that and say nice things about him.

VICTOR: ...Like what? Peter I hope you escape and stay escaped?

ANNA: If you love him like a son.

VICTOR: What about us poor bastards? Don't we count? He buggered off knowing full well we'd suffer if he did. D'you want me to thank him for it? Peter you're a selfish man who doesn't give a stuff about anyone but I love you. Thank you for getting us put on this transport to hell. But no... what am I saying? When you make us suffer like this you give us the chance to prove how much we love you. We prove it by not saying a word against you but by being pleased you've saved your skin at our expense.

MILLIE: You don't sound like you mean that.

ANNA: We all had the choice to do what Peter did.

VICTOR: Explain that to me?

ANNA: We all could've worked out a plan of escape and put it into action?

VICTOR: What nonsense. Have you seen me run or duck or weave?

ANNA: No I haven't.

VICTOR: Because I can't. I waddle... like a duck. I'm not young and fit like the rest of you. Short of someone offering me a tank as transport I couldn't have done what Peter's done in a million years. I like to think I wouldn't have tried.

MILLIE: Why not?

ANNA: Because he was thinking of others of course like he always does.

VICTOR: You're like my children. Knowing what would happen to you if I... if I... (*Gesture to include hut and them*)

MILLIE: You'll make me cry if you keep on.

VICTOR: (*To Anna*) Did Peter tell you about his plans?

ANNA: We all knew he dreamed of escaping. He's talked of nothing else for the past months.

VICTOR: A group-escape. His dream of a mighty mass breakout which no one took seriously including I think Peter himself. But sneaking away? Without a word. Unless there was...? (*Looks at Anna*)

ANNA: Not to me.

VICTOR: Anna you can say, I won't be angry. Did he tell you? Did he? Anna if you value your name, if you want me to still think of you as decent and honest, tell.

ANNA: ...Once.

VICTOR: When?

ANNA: Two days ago.

VICTOR: You didn't think to tell anyone?

ANNA: What time have I had? It's been a madhouse...

MILLIE: Did he ask you go with him? He's so in love with you I bet he begged you on bended knees.

VICTOR: Not Peter – he's a selfish person.

ANNA: He's not selfish and he did ask. (*Victor smiles as anna rises to bait*)

MILLIE: And you said no?

ANNA: I'm still here Millie so what do you think?

MILLIE: I wish he'd asked me. I'd have gone like a shot.

VICTOR: When he told you did you remind him what would happen to us if he went?

ANNA: Why would I? He knows how things here work.

VICTOR: Answer the question Anna. Did you or didn't you?

ANNA: I don't remember.

MILLIE: I bet you do you just don't want to say.

ANNA: How dare you say that? If I tell you I don't remember, I don't.

MILLIE: I'm only asking. No need to bite my head off.

VICTOR: If Peter told you he was going you had a chance to stop him. He's so soft on you it's odds on he'd've ditched his plan if you'd asked him. Especially when I know you think our best chance of success is to stay here. Did you try and stop him?

ANNA: Peter's an adult for goodness sake. He makes up his own mind. How can I change it?

VICTOR: Did you try?

MILLIE: You can at least tell us that Anna. No one's going to criticise you. Well I'm not 'specially as I'd've jumped at the chance of going... if he'd asked.

ANNA: Would you Millie? Really?

MILLIE: I think so. I hope so. No I know so.

ANNA: Until you're in the situation, you can't know.

VICTOR: You were in it Anna. For the umpteenth time did you or didn't you try to keep him here? (*Anna no answer*) Stop hiding things. Stop being this devious plotting person who's not like the Anna I've always known.

ANNA: I told him to go.

VICTOR: (*Shocked*) You did what? I can't... that's...

ANNA: He offered to stay. Not because he was worried about what would happen to his colleagues - which he was. And not because he felt guilty about them – which he did. He said he would stay on one condition - that I told him I loved him as deeply as he loved me. Nothing else would do. (*Falters*) And I couldn't... (*Millie puts an arm around anna*)

VICTOR: Sent to hell for want of a few silly words. Thanks. Considerate of you.

MILLIE: Saying you love someone if you don't isn't silly.

VICTOR: Oh well – it won't be fatal. Not for me anyway. I'm minutes away from release thank god. (*Sees CS offstage*) Ah our glorious sun-god's descending from on high. If he walks this way...

Enter CS – immaculate as usual

CS: Good evening to you all. Miss Hilmann. Anna. Gerrin. (*CS shakes their hand as he says their name*) I wanted to offer my thanks in person before you left.

VICTOR: We're honoured commandant.

CS: You'll be missed. You've livened this place up with your cabaret evenings for sure ...Have a safe journey and best wishes in your new home.

VICTOR: Thank you sir, thank you indeed. We're touched. Can I quickly ask if you have any news on my deferral?

CS: Who's dealing with it?

VICTOR: Mishen.

CS: No one better. He'll get a good result.

VICTOR: You've not heard then sir?

CS: No but why would I? There are still some things that progress here without me.

VICTOR: I've got so much to do here. If I'm sent away my project will be half-finished. How will the Camp do without me?

CS: You continue the work where you're going. They'll appreciate it I'm sure.

VICTOR: Do they have cabaret?

CS: If they don't, you request it. Like you did here.

VICTOR: But... I'm happy where I am. I feel at home here. If you could keep me I'd go down on my knees. I go down on my knees.

Victor falls on his knees

CS: Gerrin get up. This is embarrassing... (*CS helps Gerrin to his feet, no easy task*)

VICTOR: Apologies if I embarrassed you. Please help me stay. You need me. The Centre needs my experience. No one produces shows like me.

CS: I'm grateful for what you've done.

VICTOR: Thank you, thank you. The train loads soon. Once the doors shut I won't be able to get off. It would be such a relief to know before then...

CS: If you get locked on, I'll send for you...

VICTOR: I'd rather get a decision before we leave...

CS: I've told you what I'll do Gerrin. I've got a thousand travellers to take care of this morning apart from you so can you let me get on?

VICTOR: Not another word. Just my deepest thanks to a Commandant with a great big heart.

CS: (*To Millie*) Miss Hilmann, I hope you'll sing the children to sleep on the journey with that lovely voice of yours?

MILLIE: There's nothing like singing for keeping people's spirits up – nicer things being out of reach.

CS: That's the magical power of song isn't it. Anna could I have a word? Would you mind?

CS walks SR, some distance away from Victor and Millie. Anna follows him

(*Quiet voice*) I'm truly truly sorry.

ANNA: Are you?

CS: ...I phoned HQ a minute after our chat. They'd already read my report. I told them fifty times it was a mistake. 'She's blameless. There's been no spying. I forgot I told her to dust edges. She's an excellent house-cleaner.' 'If you keep on like this we'll suspect more than a director-resident relationship, Schaffer. That could have consequences.' They sent me a signed order with your name on it.

ANNA: Just mine?

CS: ...And Peter's. And Gerrin's.

ANNA: We should be flattered they know us by name.

CS: I can't ignore a signed order.

ANNA: Have you been tempted?

CS: What does it matter since I can't?

ANNA: Why can't you? Refuse to carry it out. No one can make you.

CS: D'you think I haven't thought about it? How I can get round it? What excuses I can find not to do it? I've thought of nothing else since it arrived.

ANNA: Go with your feelings – the ones you say you have for me. Be brave. At least I'd know you'd risked something to keep me here.

CS: Would you want to stay? With your mother and sister leaving?

ANNA: Give me the choice and we'll see.

CS: HQ are sharp. They sniff out the truth. A German involved with a Jew? Major offence. Misconduct charge. Reduced to the ranks, reputation wrecked, sent off to fight almost certainly die in some freezing hole on the Eastern Front.

ANNA: Is this your way of telling me you won't do anything? (*CS says nothing*) Mother and Millie – was there a signed order for them?

CS: Their names were on the Tuesday list.

ANNA:	You approve it.
CS:	I don't study every name. I count a thousand and sign it off.
ANNA:	Can't you let them stay? If you have any feelings for me don't send them. You can at least do that.
CS:	When Peter absconded he put his friends and colleagues...
ANNA:	...And their families?
CS:	...*And* their families on the next transport out. That's the rule.
ANNA:	Can't you bend it?
CS:	It's the foundation of discipline in this Camp. One person escapes, fifty suffer. If we weaken this we'll have chaos in a week. More will do what Peter's done. The camp will collapse.
ANNA:	You can alter the list. You did once...
CS:	When it was day to day.
ANNA:	You're not going to do anything then?
CS:	I hope they treat you well where you're going.
ANNA:	Have you asked them to?
CS:	What influence do I have for god sake? I'm not even sure who runs the place anymore. I've heard rumours. Orders to close camps... ship people out. Before the allies get to them...
ANNA:	So you're losing...

CS: ...So what notice is anyone going to take of me? They're bigger fish than I am. They're thinking of themselves.

ANNA: You're not going to step out of line are you Conrad? Not even for me. Not weighed against your career and the opinion of your friends...

CS: Blame me – I don't mind – it's my fault. I get angry and when I do... Of course I wouldn't've got angry if you hadn't gone through my papers but I should've kept calm... (*Thinks a bit*) ...What difference would it have made? You'd be here anyway because you worked with Peter. If only he'd stayed. I could've tweaked the list, kept you here with your mother and sister. I could've done that. Why oh why did you go through my papers?

ANNA: All my fault then.

CS: No mine. My temper. But you provoked it. When you went through my things. What a sodding mess.

ANNA: That's in the past. We need to think of now.

CS: Did you know Peter was going to escape?

ANNA: What does it matter if I did?

CS: You were with him yesterday before you came to see me.

ANNA: I didn't notice you around.

CS: One of my guards was watching you – through binoculars.

ANNA:	Did you set that up?
CS:	Well I... yes.
ANNA:	Why?
CS:	Just... I did.
ANNA:	You know Peter and I kissed then? (*CS nods*) You wouldn't know what was in the kiss. Like you didn't know what was in our kiss...?
CS:	You put a ring on Peter's finger. Was it mine?
ANNA:	No.
CS:	Where is mine?
ANNA:	I traded it for fruit for my mother.
CS:	(*After quite a silence*) It served a good purpose.
ANNA:	The best if she gets her health back.
CS:	I'll keep my fingers crossed for you. You're a wonderful artist – our nation should be proud of you.
ANNA:	Maybe they will be in a thousand years.
CS:	Thanks for the dancing. I won't forget it.

Anna looks long at CS

She walks back to Victor and Millie. Sits on floor with them

CS follows Anna to the group

CS:	When I look at what's happening to you artists today you know what I think? We need more trust in this world.
MILLIE:	More trust and more love.

VICTOR: I think – if I may say – we have trust. I see it all around.

CS: But enough d'you think...?

VICTOR: You trust me to put on shows. Why? Because I've shown I'll put on the sort of show you like.

CS: Yes... that's trust.

ANNA: By putting on our shows we pretended things were normal here when we knew they weren't. When we gave our evenings of laughter and romance and high-leg kicking we helped to hide the truth. We broke the higher trust we owed our audience.

VICTOR: What nonsense Anna. Everyone needs a bit of escapism, wherever they are. She doesn't mean it. (*To Anna*) You don't mean that Anna.

ANNA: I do. We should be ashamed.

VICTOR: That's completely the wrong way to look at things.

CS: I see Miss Hilmann's point.

VICTOR: Yes of course so do I. There are always two sides to every question, or even more... thank you, thank you for everything you've done for me... us. And will do in the not too distant future... (*Knowing look*)

CS: I'm only sorry I couldn't have kept you here longer. Goodbye. And good luck. And have a great future. All of you. I'll miss you. (*Looking sadly at Anna*) Very much.

CS exits

MILLIE: What did you talk about?

ANNA: Nothing.

MILLIE: It looked a lot of words for nothing.

VICTOR: Anna d'you want to wreck my life? It's all very well you speaking your mind but every time you do my chances of a deferral nosedive.

ANNA: You didn't agree with me on anything. He could see that.

VICTOR: If you put him in a bad mood it certainly can't help me can it?

ANNA: I wouldn't want to harm your chances Victor. If I have I apologise.

MILLIE: Here's Mum Anna. (*Calling to someone off*) We're her daughters. We'll take over. Thank you.

ANNA: Victor can you help?

ETTE: (*Off*) ...Ooh... I don't have a good bone left in my body. I'm a bruised woman.

Exit Anna and Millie

VICTOR: ...Mishen, hurry up. You promised you wouldn't leave it till the last minute you rat. What're you playing at?

Re-enter Anna and Millie supporting Ette, one on each side. Ette groans

ANNA: We'll be very careful Mum.

ETTE: Mind my back. It's broken in at least two places. Those young men took no notice of my groans.

ANNA: We'll take you up to the train and lift you gently into the carriage.

ETTE: Hmph. You call that a carriage? More like a cattle-truck.

ANNA: I'll hold Mum under her shoulders. Victor can you take her legs?

MILLIE: I can take Mum's legs. Victor you support her middle. (*Victor does as he's asked*)

ANNA: On the count of three – one, two, three, lift.

The three swing Ette as gently as they can into the cattle-truck

ETTE: Oh my poor benighted bones. I ache all over.

MILLIE: Once we get you settled they'll ease.

ETTE: How can I settle surrounded with people I don't know? I'm the wife of a university lecturer. I used to travel first class.

MILLIE: Just be friendly and they'll be friendly back.

ETTE: But who are they? I'm not used to mixing with people whose names I don't know.

ANNA: Whoever they are I'm sure they're all nice.

ETTE: How will I stretch? I have to you know. Doctor's orders. I'm sure you can't budge in these trucks when they're full.

ANNA: We'll stay near you and clear some space.

ETTE: ...As to what we're all going to smell like in three days...

MILLIE: We'll smell sweet. We'll pretend we've splashed the most expensive perfume on. Gallons of it. Chanel for you Mum, Joy for me and Scandal for Anna.

ANNA: Lovely idea Millie. I'll use so much perfume.

ETTE: I wouldn't be surprised if I've lost my sense of smell, the battering my sense-buds have had since I came to this place.

MILLIE: Your Chanel smells like crushed rose petals with a hint of lemon.

ANNA: The scent of early morning in a meadow in spring.

ETTE: (*Breathes gently*) ...It's coming back ...I can smell it... mmm...

VICTOR: Where's that Mishen? What's he playing at? It'll be too late soon. Hurry up you lazy good for nothing. He's got my mother's wedding ring as a down payment.

ETTE: You shouldn't give that man anything as precious as that. And certainly not till he's delivered the goods. He's a thief and a liar.

VICTOR: It's all I had left. I was desperate.

ETTE: You kept it till last because it's more than a ring to a faithful son like you. It's your mother. Her happy day. Her memory.

VICTOR: I've never felt so bad as when I handed it over to the worm.

ETTE: It's just money to him. The fact it's precious to you means nothing.

VICTOR: What could I do? He does nothing for nothing.

ETTE: You're wrong there. He normally does nothing for something. Are you getting in daughters?

MILLIE: Last breath of fresh air.

ANNA: (STARING OFF) Well look who's arrived. The star of the show. Like some lord of darkness sweeping down from on high on the humble plebs. The tremor that sweeps the crowd as he makes his grand entrance.

CS appears, immaculately dressed. Suit, gloves, hat, polished boots as before

Sound fx voices: "Everybody on board" " No more dawdling now" "On you get or my boot up your arse" "Stop that kid screaming"

Anna, Millie climb into truck

VOICE OFF: In you get Gerrin.

VICTOR: I'm waiting for Mishen. He's got my deferral.

VOICE OFF: Like he's got a thousand other people's. Get on or we'll throw you on. You wouldn't want to visit that on your fellow passengers would you? (*Laughs*)

VICTOR: But I'm not meant to be going.

VOICE OFF: Last warning Gerrin. Not even your jokes'll save you now.

VICTOR: I'll see you lose your job young man. (*Fx off of young man laughing*) You'll be on a Tuesday excursion before too long.

Victor clambers into freight truck, helped by Anna & Millie

CS walks past

ANNA: Go on great Director. Disobey. Show you've got some spirit.

VICTOR: Help me sir, please help.

CS waves, slight smile as walks along platform

MILLIE: Just like royalty.

ANNA: Get us off Conrad. If you've got any feelings for me.

Exit CS

VICTOR: ...Why didn't I do what Peter did? Why aren't I fitter? Why am I so timid? If the worst comes to the worst, CS'll send for me. I'll no sooner get there than I'll be on my way back. Hurry up Mishen you thief, you've got enough of my money.

MILLIE: What song shall we sing first?

ANNA: 'To Me You're Beautiful'?

MILLIE: Followed by 'I know Some Day a Miracle Will Happen'. I'm excited... (*Feels her pocket*) My crystals are in a safe place. They'll help us.

VICTOR: They're shutting the doors. Mishen get a move on. What are you playing at? Get a bloody move on you weasel, you swine, you useless specimen.

Sound fx: truck door sliding shut. Bolt slams over

Then another, then another, and another, and another.

Sound fx: train whistle. Steam train crawling out of centre

Sound fx: female voices singing faintly heard: 'To me you're beautiful'

Lights slowly fade to black.

END OF SCENE 12

SCENE 13

Spot up. CS at his table. Picks up phone. Dials. Waits

CS: ...Aus der Funten's office pease. (*He waits*) Schaffer here sir. It's about Anna Hilmann yes *the* Anna Hilmann, the cabaret dancer yes. She left on this morning's transport. Can she be brought back? I explained in the note I sent... (*And start to fade lights*) Resign? No I... don't feel that strongly... I love my job. I just thought... it seems... I'll leave it then shall I? No of course. Sorry if I've um... been a nuisance. Thank you for listening sir. I will sir. Thank you...

Sound fx: Leo Fuld sings 'hebrew chant'

Fx: lights fade

THE END